MYSTERIES OF THE ROSARY

Illustrated with Master Artists Paintings

William R. Parks

Hershey Books

Dedication:
To fellow travelers on our journey toward Heaven.

www.wrparks.com

ISBN: 978-0-88493-068-6

Published by Hershey Books

Cover artwork by Bartolomé
Esteban Murillo (1617-1682) Virgin
and Child with a Rosary

CONTENTS

THE FIVE SORROWFUL MYSTERIES

THE FIVE GLORIOUS MYSTERIES

PRAYERS OF THE ROSARY

While holding the crucifix of the rosary make the Sign of the Cross and say the Apostles' Creed:

In the name of the Father, and of the Son, and of the Holy Spirit. Amen.

Then say the Apostle's Creed:

I believe in God, the Father Almighty, Creator of Heaven and earth; and in Jesus Christ, His only Son Our Lord, Who was conceived by the Holy Spirit, born of the Virgin Mary, suffered under Pontius Pilate, was crucified, died, and was buried. He descended into Hell; the third day He rose again from the dead; He ascended into Heaven, and sitteth at the right hand of God, the Father almighty; from thence He shall come to judge the living and the dead. I believe in the Holy Spirit, the holy Catholic Church, the communion of saints, the forgiveness of sins, the resurrection of the body and life everlasting. Amen.

On the first single bead after the crucifix (and on all single beads of the rosary) say the Lord's prayer:

Our Father, Who art in heaven, Hallowed be Thy Name. Thy Kingdom come. Thy Will be done, on earth as it is in Heaven. Give us this day our daily bread. And forgive us our trespasses, as we forgive those who trespass against us. And lead us not into temptation, but deliver us from evil. Amen.

On each of the next three beads say the Hail Mary and ask to increase your virtues of Faith, Hope and Charity. Follow it with the Glory Be prayer.

Hail Mary, full of grace, the Lord is with thee; Blessed art thou among women and blessed is the fruit of thy womb, Jesus. Holy Mary, Mother of God, pray for us sinners, now and at the hour of our death. Amen.

Glory be to the Father, and to the Son, and to the Holy Spirit. As it was in the beginning, is now, and ever shall be, world without end. Amen

Before starting the first decade meditate on the first mystery and then pray the Our Father on the single bead followed by praying a Hail Mary on each of the ten beads following the large bead.

After praying a decade, say the Glory Be and pray the Fatima invocation:

O myJesus, forgive us our sins, save us from the fires of hell, and lead all souls to heaven, especially those in most need of thy mercy. At the conclusion of the last decade say the Hail Holy Queen prayer.

Hail Holy Queen, mother of mercy; our life, our sweetness, and our hope. To thee do we cry, poor banished children of Eve. To thee do we send up our sighs, mourning and weeping in this vale of tears. Turn, then, most gracious advocate, thine eyes of mercy toward us. And after this, our exile, show unto us the blessed fruit of thy womb, Jesus. O clement, O loving, O sweet Virgin Mary. Pray for us, O holy Mother of God, that we may be made worthy of the promises of Christ. Amen.

15 PROMISES FOR PRAYING THE ROSARY

The following 15 promises concerning praying the Rosary were given by Our Lady to St. Dominic and Blessed Alain:

1) Whoever shall faithfully serve me by the recitation of the Rosary, shall receive signal graces.

2) I promise my special protection and the greatest graces to all those who shall recite the Rosary.

3) The Rosary shall be a powerful armor against hell, it will destroy vice, decrease sin, and defeat heresies.

4) The Rosary will cause virtue and good works to flourish; it will obtain for souls the abundant mercy of God; it will withdraw the hearts of men from the love of the world and its vanities, and will lift them to the desire for eternal things. Oh, that souls would sanctify themselves by this means.

5) The soul which recommends itself to me by the recitation of the Rosary, shall not perish.

6) Whoever shall recite the Rosary devoutly, applying himself to the consideration of its sacred mysteries shall never be conquered by misfortune. God will not chastise him in His justice, he shall not perish by an unprovided death; if he be just he shall remain in the grace of God, and become worthy of eternal life.

7) Whoever shall have a true devotion for the Rosary shall not die without the sacraments of the Church.

8) Those who are faithful to recite the Rosary shall have during their life and at their death the light of God and the plenititude of His graces; at the moment of death they shall participate in the merits of the saints in paradise.

9) I shall deliver from Purgatory those who have been devoted to the Rosary.

10) The faithful children of the Rosary shall merit a high degree of glory in Heaven.

11) You shall obtain all you ask of me by the recitation of the Rosary.

12) All those who propagate the Holy Rosary shall be aided by me in their necessities.

13) I have obtained from my Divine Son that all the advocates of the Rosary shall have for intercessors the entire celestial court during their life and at the hour of death.

14) All who recite the Rosary are my sons and daughters, and brothers and sisters of my only Son Jesus Christ.

15) Devotion of my Rosary is a great sign of predestination.

The Five Joyful Mysteries

1st The Annunciation to the Blessed Virgin Mary. Painting by Leonardo DaVinci.

The angel Gabriel was sent from God unto a city of Galilee, named Nazareth to a virgin espoused to a man whose name was Joseph, of the house of David, and the virgin's name was Mary. And the angel came and said, Hail, thou art highly favoured, the Lord is with thee: blessed art thou among women. Thou shalt conceive in thy womb, and bring forth a son, and shalt call His name "Yeshua" which is the Hebrew word for salvation! And Mary said, behold the handmaid of the Lord, be it done unto me according to thy word. The second person of the Holy Trintiy became man in Jesus Christ who is son of God and son of Mary!

2nd **The Visitation.** Painting by Jacques Daret.

Mary, pregnant with Jesus, visited her cousin Elizabeth, who was also pregnant with John the Baptist.

When Elizabeth heard Mary's greeting, the child leaped in her womb and Elizabeth was filled with the Holy Spirit. Elizabeth told Mary she was the most blessed of all women and blessed is the fruit of Mary's womb.

Elizabeth expressed humility asking why she should be so honored with a visit from mother of her Lord. Mary replied in humility that the Lord, her Savior looked upon this lowly handmaiden who will be called blessed for all generations to come.

3rd The Nativity of our Lord, Jesus Christ.
Painting by Sandro Botticelli.

A government decree was made requiring people to go to their ancestral home and be registered.

Mary and Joseph went to Bethlehem but were unable to find a room at the inn. They were offered a stable. The Son of God, our Savior, Jesus Christ, King of Kings was born as a pauper in a stable.

An angel of the Lord appeared to shepherds nearby and asked them to visit their Savior.

4th The Presentation of Baby Jesus in the Temple. Painting by Ambrogio Lorenzetti.

Obeying the Law of Moses where the first born is consecrated to the Lord, the parents took baby Jesus to the Temple. Prompted by the Holy Spirit, Simeon, a devout man, took Jesus into his arms and said his eyes have now seen salvation.

5th The Finding of the Boy Jesus in the Temple.
Painting by William Holmes Hunt.

During a visit to Jerusalem the boy, Jesus, stayed behind without Mary and Joseph. After three days of looking for Jesus, they found him in the Temple conversing with learned religious leaders. Mary asked Jesus, why have you done this? Jesus answered that He must be about His Father's business.

Jesus then went with his parents to Nazareth where He remained under their care. Jesus helped his foster father Joseph in the carpentry business until He was 30 and then Jesus began his public ministry offering salvation to the world.

The Five Luminous Mysteries

1st The Baptism of Jesus in the Jordon River.
Painting by Piero Della Francesca.

    Jesus came to the Jordan River and was baptized by John, the Baptist. After He was baptized the Spirit of God descended on Jesus like a dove. A voice from Heaven said, "This is my beloved Son, in whom I am well pleased."

2nd The Wedding Feast at Cana. Painting by Maerten de Vos.

Jesus, his mother and disciples were invited to a wedding feast at Cana, and the wine ran out. Mary told Jesus they ran out of wine. Jesus asked the servants to fill some containers with water. He performed His first public miracle and changed the water into very fine tasting wine.

3rd The Proclamation of the Kingdom of God.
Painting by anonymous artist from Westphalia.

Jesus proclaimed the Kingdom of God.
Judgement is assigned to Jesus. He will judge all
people. The good news is that forgiveness of sins is
available for those who repent.

4th The Transfiguration of Jesus Christ. Painting by Raphael.

Jesus led his apostles up a high mountain and changed His appearance into a glorified body to show them that He is King of Kings and Lord of Lords. Moses and Elijah appeared with Jesus. This miraculous event prepared the apostles for the coming arrest, passion and death of Jesus.

5th The Last Supper. Restored painting of Leonardo Da Vinci.

At the Last Supper, Jesus said to his apostles, "One of you will betray me." He told them, "He that dipped his hand with me in the dish, the same shall betray me." It was Judas who betrayed him.

As they were eating, Jesus blessed bread and gave thanks and broke it and gave it to his apostles and said, "Take, eat, this is my body given for you. Do this in remembrance of me." He also took a cup of wine and said, "This is my blood which is shed for many." He referred to the Crucifixion he was about to suffer to atone for sins of mankind.

The Last Supper provides the basis for "Holy Communion" also known as the "Eucharist." The bread and wine are consecrated and become the body and blood of Jesus Christ and are shared.

The Five Sorrowful Mysteries

1st Agony in the Garden. Painting by Heinrich Hofmann.

After the Last Supper, Jesus went to the Mount of Olives and prayed, in anticipation of His coming crucifixion, saying, "Father, if thou be willing, remove this cup from me: nevertheless not my will, but thine, be done." Being in agony as He prayed His sweat was as it were great drops of blood falling down to the ground.

2ⁿᵈ Scourging at the Pillar. Painting by William-Adolphe Bouguereau.

The chief priests and elders of the people plotted against Jesus to put him to death. They bound him, and delivered him to Pontius Pilate, the governor. Pilate had Jesus delivered to his soldiers to be scourged and crucified.

3rd **Crowning with Thorns.** Painting by Caravaggio.

   The soldiers stripped Jesus and clothed Him with purple, and put a crown of thorns about his head and made fun of Him and began to salute Him, "Hail, King of the Jews!" They spit on Him, and bowed their knees and worshipped Him.

   After they mocked Jesus, they took off the purple from Him, and put his own clothes on Him, and led Him out to be crucified.

   We are very unhappy with the way Jesus. our Lord, was treated by Roman soldiers. We should always strive to help withdraw those thorns by offering our prayers and sacrifices for the salvation of sinners. Amen.

4th Jesus Carrying the Cross. Painting by Raphael.

Jesus was given a cross to carry to His crucifixion site, Golgotha. Along the way He met His Mother Mary. He fell down and Simon of Cyrene helped Jesus carry the cross. Women of Jerusalem were weeping. Veronica wiped the face of Jesus.

5th The Crucifixion. Painting by Diego Adele.

Jesus so loved us people that He humbled himself and became obedient unto death. He died on the cross for our sins so that we might be forgiven.

The Five Glorious Mysteries

1st The Resurrection. Painting by Noel Coypel.

Very early in the morning Mary Magdalene came to the sepulcher of Jesus. But the stone was rolled away from the door. Inside a young man was sitting and he said to her, "Do not be afraid. Jesus of Nazareth who was crucified has risen."

2nd The Ascension. Painting by John Singleton Copley.

And it came to pass, Jesus showed Himself to be alive. He blessed His followers and then He was carried up to Heaven. They worshipped Him and returned to Jerusalem with great joy. And were continually in the temple, praising and blessing God. Amen.

3rd Pentecost – Descent of the Holy Spirit.
Painting by Duccio di Buoninsegna.

When the day of Pentecost came, the apostles and Mary were all in one place. Suddenly there came a sound from heaven as of a rushing mighty wind, and it filled the house where they were sitting.

There appeared unto them tongues of fire, and it sat upon each of them. They were all filled with the Holy Spirit, and began to speak in other languages, as the Spirit gave them speech.

When this noise was heard, a multitude came together, and were confounded, because every man heard them speak in his own language. They were all amazed.

May the inspiration of the Holy Spirit fill the hearts and minds of people on earth! Amen!

4ᵗʰ The Assumption of Mary to Heaven. Painting by Peter Paul Rubens.

At the end of her earthly life, the Mother of Jesus, our Blessed Virgin Mary, was taken up bodily to Heaven.

5th The Coronation of Mary in Heaven. Painting by Peter Paul Rubens.

There appeared a great wonder in heaven; a woman clothed with the sun, and the moon under her feet, and upon her head a crown of twelve stars. And she brought forth a male child, who was to rule all nations with a rod of iron: and her child was caught up unto God, and to his throne.

More information about our below books is listed at **www.wrparks.com** and sold by **www.amazon.com**. Post title and author's name in the Amazon search box to obtain detailed information concerning each of these books.

Windows to Heaven
Through the Heart of a Lion
Peace In The Storms of Life 30 Day Devotional
Prayers from the Heart
Marriage – Yesterday, Today, Always
Made in America
We Remember the Day of President Kennedy's Assassination
The Occupation of Korea – An American Soldiers Experience
Political Economy and The Payment of Labor
The Joyful Cook's Guide To Heavenly Greek Cuisine
Handbook for Piano Practice
Piano Practice for the Advancing Student
Program Your Calculator
Letters to a Young Math Teacher
Letters to a Young Classroom Teacher
Beginning Algebra
Sets, Numbers and Flowcharts
Introduction to Logic
Computer Number Bases
1 + 1 = 1 An Introduction to Boolean Algebra and Switching Circuits
Introduction to Gambling Theory – Know the odds
Birder's Break
Birds and Birdwatchers
The Nature Watch Collection Book One
The Nature Watch Collection Book Two
Earth, God's Garden
Living with Heart Arrhythmias
Children's Books:
The Calico Caterpillar
Animal Alphabet: Fun Facts
Animal Tails
Choices
Time to Fly
Jonah The Reluctant Prophet
Peppi Puffin to the Rescue

Made in the USA
Monee, IL
03 March 2021